The Girls' Book of Friendship

COOL QUOTES, TRUE
STORIES, SECRETS,
AND MORE

Edited by Catherine Dee

Megan Tingley Books

Little, Brown and Company
BOSTON   NEW YORK   LONDON

To my best girlfriends: Mom, Vicky,
Sarah, and Jessie

Compilation copyright © 2001 by Catherine Dee
Illustrations copyright © 2001 by Ali Douglass

First Edition

Acknowledgments of permission to reprint
previously published material appear on page 191.

Library of Congress Cataloging-in-Publication Data

The girls' book of friendship : cool quotes, true stories, secrets, and more / edited by Catherine Dee. — 1st ed.
       p.   cm.
    Includes index.
    ISBN 0-316-16818-1
  1. Friendship — Quotations, maxims, etc. — Juvenile literature.
[1. Friendship — Quotations, maxims, etc.   2. Women —
Quotations.   3. Quotations.]
I. Dee, Catherine.   II. Title.

PN6084.F8 G57 2001
177'.62 — dc21   00-067620

10 9 8 7 6 5 4 3 2 1

LAK

Printed in the United States of America

Acknowledgments

This celebration of friendship was made possible by all the girls and women who contributed their inspirational stories and quotes! Special thanks to Megan Tingley for seeing this book's possibilities, along with my editor, Mary Gruetzke, and Will Gordon at Little, Brown. Thanks to my best friend, Jonathan Ganz, for his great suggestions and support. Appreciation to Elizabeth Carlassare, Sarah Dee, Brooke Hodess, Molly Griffiths, Monica Johnson, Tami Rush, Whitney Stenberg, and Christine Szeto, who read the manuscript. Thanks to researchers Jeanie Fraser, Lorre Leon Mendelson, Pat Guy, Christine Mackie, and the Redwood City Public Library staff. Other helpers included Holly Audley, Gabrielle Bamford, Emily Daly, Bridget Goodrich, Nancy Gruver, Barbara Handler, Christine Sanders Jump, Meg Moulton, Patricia Ogren, Whitney Ransome, M. J. Reale, Cynthia Showalter, Jo Lynn Smith, Ann Stoffel, and Patricia C. Ungar. Finally, thanks to Mom, Dad, Vicky, Sarah, and Ryan, along with Dick, Hal, Charley, and Mike—for all their love and encouragement.

Contents

Introduction

My best friend has taught me in numerous ways and opened my eyes. . . . You hold my best friend in your hand. My best friend is that rarest of jewel . . . a book.   —MICHELE H. LACINA, WRITER

Welcome to *The Girls' Book of Friendship!*

This book can help you:

- Evaluate whether someone would make a good friend
- Become the kind of friend everyone needs
- Know when you can truly trust someone
- Make friends in unexpected places
- Become an attentive listener
- Maintain friendships in and outside of the popular crowd
- Plan adventures you'll never forget
- Appreciate the value of friendship
- Inspire and be inspired by your friends
- . . . and much more

The Girls' Book of Friendship has thirty chapters, each dedicated to a different aspect of life with your friends. You'll find a combination of different elements in these chapters:

Cool Quotes about all facets of friendship. The wise girls and women who've said these bits of wisdom hail from assorted countries, occupations, and historical periods. These writers, actors, singers, professionals in different fields, and "regular" people offer great insights based on their own experiences. If you're having trouble with a friend, a quote about fights could help you make up. You might read a quote about best friends that gives you a new appreciation for your own; or one about celebrating friends that inspires you to plan a friendship "anniversary" lunch. This book puts it all at your fingertips so you can find the right ideas and suggestions about friendship any time you need them.

True Stories. These tales are warm and wonderful, intriguing and eye-opening. You'll eavesdrop on what it was like when someone lost her best friend's trust, or realized a new friend could be a *best* friend, or reconnected with someone who moved away. These life "snapshots" capture incidents that affected the writers' feelings about friendship or their beliefs in general.

Poems. These assorted short works pay tribute to being your own best friend, old and new friends, friends who are always there, and more.

Pal Projects. Here's where you'll find creative ways to let friends know how much you care and to document your relationships.

Quick Lists. These at-a-glance lists cover such topics as qualities people look for in friends, good movies to watch together, and what to expect at sleepovers.

FRIENDLY FACTS. This section includes interesting facts and figures on how people think about friendship.

While you'll find plenty of helpful facts and suggestions in *The Girls' Book of Friendship,* keep in mind that it's not supposed to be an all-inclusive "textbook" on how to make and keep

friends. This book is instead a *celebration* of what friendship—
and especially female friendship—is all about. I hope it will
help you celebrate and enjoy life with your friends—now
and for years to come!

Catherine Dee

Chapter 1

Terms of Endearment

 *It sounds like a silly question, but do you know what the word "friend" means?*

One definition is "a person who cares deeply about you and shows it." A friend can be in your family or outside it, living nearby or hundreds of miles away; but she's distinguished herself because of the way she treats you.

A friend is so much more, though. Check out the quotes on the following pages and then make up a definition of your own.

Cool Quotes

A friend is someone who sees through you and still enjoys the view.

—WILMA ASKINAS, WRITER

Friends are pretty much everything, the squish in our organs, the crinkles in our smiling faces, the decadent fun in shared adventures and secret promises.

—LISA KENNEDY MONTGOMERY ("KENNEDY"),
TV VIDEO JOCKEY AND HOST, SPEAKER

I've always looked at friends as the family we choose.

—JOAN LUNDEN, TV HOST

Friendships are like a boat in a stormy sea, and whoever else is in the boat is that much more important because they are sharing the turmoil of adolescence with you.

— DEE SHEPHERD-LOOK, PROFESSOR

Friendship ought to be a gratuitous joy, like the joys afforded by art, or life.

— SIMONE WEIL, PHILOSOPHER, 1909–1943

Friendship is a heart-flooding feeling that can happen to any two people who are caught up in the act of being themselves, together.

— LETTY COTTIN POGREBIN, WRITER

Female friendship is most of all about sharing who we are. . . . It doesn't matter to me what I do with my friend, as long as I am with her.

— JANET F. QUINN, NURSE, PROFESSOR, RESEARCHER

A good friend is a connection to life—a tie to the past, a road to the future, the key to sanity in a totally insane world.

— LOIS WYSE, PHOTOGRAPHER, WRITER

Friends Forgive When Friends Forget

Susie and I have known each other since we were nine. A few years ago she was in a hospital across the country. I called her every day. It was hard for me because she kept forgetting I'd called. I was worried, but the nurse reassured me that her memory loss was just a side effect of her medication.

I asked the nurse to put a notepad on her bedside table. We continued our conversations, and before we'd hang up I'd tell her to write "Bobbi called today" on the notepad.

At the end of this worrisome week I went to visit her. When I walked into her hospital room, the stack of notes was on the bedside table. She told me she hadn't realized how scared she was. She grabbed the notes and exclaimed, "These kept me from feeling lonely!" We cried. In that moment I realized how special our friendship is. And despite the fact that we live apart, neither of us has felt lonely since.

—ALDEN (BOBBI) DEAN, POET

FRIENDLY FACT

Most friendships are formed between people who are about the same age and have similar backgrounds.

Chapter 2

The Power of Pals

In ancient Greece, people considered friendship (at least between men) to be more important than marriage.

The Greeks were certainly on to something. Most people who have good friends would agree that friendship is every bit as important as romantic love.

And that's not all. Studies show that having friends in your life can help you stay healthy, feel less stressed, develop more self-confidence, and even live longer. Some experts add that for teens in particular, having good friends is more important than being popular or getting good grades.

Study results aside, anyone who's ever had a close friend knows the truth: Friends can rock your world!

Cool Quotes

The first rule of life is: Cherish your friends and your family as if your life depended on it . . . because it does.

—ANN RICHARDS, POLITICIAN

If you have nothing in life but a great friend, you're rich.

—MICHELLE KWAN, FIGURE SKATER

Girlfriends aren't a luxury (though they sure feel like one!). They are a healthy necessity.

—SUSAN BRANCH, WRITER, ARTIST

Winning has always meant much to me, but winning friends has meant the most.

—BABE DIDRIKSON ZAHARIAS, ATHLETE, 1914–1956

When all is said and done, it is the people in your life, the friendships you form and the commitments you maintain, that give shape to your life.

— HILLARY RODHAM CLINTON, U.S. SENATOR

We're communal creatures, we can't do it all by ourselves. . . . We each need to find three or four or six or twelve people and meet with them once a week.

— GLORIA STEINEM, WOMEN'S RIGHTS ACTIVIST, WRITER

Friends and good manners will carry you where money won't go.

— MARGARET WALKER, WRITER, EDUCATOR, 1915–1998

The best thing to hold on to in this world is each other.

— LINDA ELLERBEE, BROADCAST JOURNALIST

Facing the Music

All my friend Dee would talk about was how she wanted to be a recognized musician. More than anything, she wanted to go to Nashville and sing and write country songs.

My dad had always told me, "If you have a dream, no matter what it is, pursue it with all your heart and soul, and you'll get there." My friend was absolutely consistent in what she wanted, and I was absolutely consistent in my answer: "Go for it, somehow, just go for it!"

One day I got a letter from her that basically said, "If it hadn't been for you telling me to go for my dream, I wouldn't be where I am today. I'm writing to thank you for believing in me and supporting me over the years. I've moved to Nashville and made a demo tape."

I cried because I never imagined I could make such a difference in someone else's life.

—JEANNE-MARIE MOORE, SOCIAL WORKER, CIVIC ACTIVIST

A Song

(written in her fifteenth year)

Life is but a troubled ocean,
Hope a meteor, love a flower
Which blossoms in the morning beam,
And withers with the evening hour.

Ambition is a dizzy height,
And glory, but a lightning gleam;
Fame is a bubble, dazzling bright,
Which fairest shines in fortune's beam.

When clouds and darkness veil the skies,
And sorrow's blast blows loud and chill,
Friendship shall like a rainbow rise,
And softly whisper—peace, be still.

—LUCRETIA MARIA DAVIDSON, POET, 1808-1825

FRIENDLY FACT

Eighty-one percent of the people surveyed in a Roper poll said their friends are in some way an expression of themselves.

Chapter 3

A Friend Is Born

You've probably seen those stick-on name tags people wear at social events that say, "Hello! My name is . . ." Pretty dorky-looking, but they serve a purpose—helping people make friends.

If you're shy about meeting people, don't despair. Try this: Whenever you see someone you'd like to know, pretend you're at one of those events and the other person wants to make friends, too. Start a conversation. It may not be the most comfortable experience, but it won't take long to find out if it was worth it. If not, no big loss—mix and mingle some more!

If you feel like you already have enough friends, rethink. Why limit the possibilities? You never know which soulmates you might miss if you don't make an effort to get to know them.

Say, "Hello! My name is . . ." to some new friends today.

Cool Quotes

Friends can be said to "fall in like" with as profound a thud as romantic partners fall in love.

—LETTY COTTIN POGREBIN, WRITER

The best time to make friends is before you need them.

—ETHEL BARRYMORE, ACTOR, 1879–1959

There are always going to be people who will like you for the wrong reasons. Your job is to find the people who like you for what you are.

—SUSAN SARANDON, ACTOR

Old Neighbors, New Friends

One summer day, my sister, my best friend, and I were picking wild roses for our mothers across the road from our elderly neighbors' white farmhouse.

The neighbors, Reid and Isabell, were out on their front porch. "We could pick some for them," I said. We arranged a nice bouquet and walked up their driveway. Isabell seemed thrilled that we'd thought of her.

I enjoyed our visit so much that the following day I went back. My visits became quite regular. I helped her can applesauce, green beans, peaches, and tomatoes that summer. Some afternoons I watched her work on patchwork quilts while she told me stories of the old days.

Her husband, Reidie, was full of jokes. He would say, "Isabell and Stephanie . . . they make a good pair. They're about the same age and the same size!" And

Isabell replied, "Well, we both have a seven in it." She was seventy-two, I was seven.

— STEPHANIE CAFARO, 11, FROM *STONE SOUP*

Off and Running

The seeds of friendship were planted the day I glanced out my window and watched my neighbor Michele lacing up her running shoes. My mind painted a picture of Michele becoming slim and physically fit while I turned into a blubbery blimp. Swallowing some kind of bashful false pride, I went outside. She asked if I wanted to run with her. I didn't have proper running shoes; and, worse yet, I was a smoker. But off we went to run-walk-walk-run-walk-walk.

Gradually we ran more than we walked, and we began talking like old friends. It was very difficult to quit smoking, but I liked Michele and our running more than cigarettes. So I stopped. After that, I not only kept up with her, but our friendship bloomed. Now I tell her she is the *M* of me and the *W* of we.

—CHERYL RAY, SAILOR, WRITER

Moment of Truth

There was a new girl at school who was not very attractive, dressed like a boy, and didn't have a lot of self-confidence. One day at lunch everyone was making fun of her, and they made her cry. Someone asked her who her friends were, and she pointed to the girl next to her, who just rolled her eyes and said, "No, I'm not." That made her cry even more.

One day she asked if I was her friend. I was surrounded by my friends and their boyfriends. I answered, "Yes, I am your friend."

After that, people no longer made fun of her, and she held her head high. And she made a lot of friends.

I've always heard that "It's not how you look on the outside, it's what's on the inside," but now I understand it. And now I have more friends than ever.

—DARA INGRAM, 11

Pal Project: Get an E-Pal

When it comes to making friends, you aren't limited to your own neighborhood, school, or town—the whole planet is fair game. Investigate these pen pal programs for girls:

- A Girl's World: www.agirlsworld.com/geri/penpal/
- Girl Zone: www.girlzone.com/html/writeher.html
- Girls Internationally Writing Letters (GIRL): www.worldkids.net/girl/

- *New Moon: The Magazine for Girls and Their Dreams*. For a list of possible pen pals, send a self-addressed, stamped envelope to Pen Pals, *New Moon*, P.O. Box 3620, Duluth, MN 55803-3620.

FRIENDLY FACT

A poll by *Twist* magazine asked girls how they would feel if their best friend was wild about a new buddy. The result: 28 percent would be curious and want to meet her; 28 percent would be nervous that they might get burned; 25 percent thought they'd get along; and 19 percent wouldn't care whether they liked her or not.

Chapter 4

That Fateful Day

 Do you remember meeting your best friend? Maybe you turned to the person sitting next to you on the first day of kindergarten and things took off from there. Or you were next-door neighbors who discovered that you had the same kind of tricycle, and, as it turned out, the same ideas for how to have fun.

Many people say they knew immediately when they met someone who was a future close friend. Others marvel at how talking to someone new seemed so comfortable, like they already knew the person.

Of course, maybe you weren't all that impressed when you met your friend; maybe you didn't even like each other. That's okay, too. But regardless of the way you met, it's lucky that your paths crossed!

Cool Quotes

Our friendship has roots as deep as if we'd known each other for a lifetime; it needed only a chance encounter for it to begin.

— CHERRY JONES, ACTOR

Two may talk together under one roof for many years, yet never really meet; and two others at first speech are old friends.

— MARY CATHERWOOD, WRITER, 1847–1901

You can tell a good friend when you meet one.

— MERON HAILE, 11

You meet your friend, your face brightens—you have struck gold.

— KASSIA, BYZANTINE POET, CA. 810–CA. 867

I wish there was some kind of agency that you could simply go to, write down all your requested characteristics in a best friend, and find a best friend. . . . Friendship is something that evolves over time, not overnight.

—STEPHANIE TUNG, 13

Banding Together

I never would have met two of my best friends if it hadn't been for an instrument. One day Ms. Ami, our fifth-grade band teacher, asked if I would like to join her and two other girls for a group flute lesson after school. I took her up on her offer and found myself playing with Ellen and Kristina, two best friends whom I didn't know that well. I soon nudged my way into their tiny group and their duet became our trio.

—CARRINGTON CROFT, 12

The Friendship Matchmaker

One of my friends, Lara, kept telling me, "You *have* to meet my friend Sal—she's just like you!" I avoided meeting Sal because I figured, "Why would I like someone just like me?" Then one day another of Sal's friends brought her over to my house. Lara was right: I liked her immediately! We have been best friends ever since.

—SARAH DEE, NONPROFIT ORGANIZATION MANAGER

A Hidden Gem

She was always the one who sat
　　　　　alone
　　　　　at lunch.
She was the one who walked
around

the playground by herself.
No one asked her to play with them
because it wasn't
cool.
We all just watched her walk by
in the playground,
moving her lips
soundlessly,
to words of her own.
She wrote herself letters.
She worked alone on her projects.
She called herself on the phone.
She had no friends.
Until one day,
when I asked her to play.

—NORA JOHNSON, 13

FRIENDLY FACT

In a magazine survey, half of the people said they liked their best friend the first time they met.

Chapter 5

Finders, Keepers

Have you ever had a friend who glommed onto you when she was down but disappeared when her life was breezing along? Or one who was only there for you in your sunny moments?

Nobody needs a "friend" like that. Unfortunately, girls sometimes don't realize that they deserve better, and they settle for whomever comes along acting halfway decent.

Keep your eyes peeled for friends who make your life exciting. If you spot someone who exhibits any of the characteristics on the next few pages, grab 'em!

Cool Quotes

The friend who holds your hand and says the wrong thing is made of dearer stuff than the one who stays away.

—BARBARA KINGSOLVER, WRITER

Lots of people want to ride with you in the limo, but what you want is someone who will take the bus with you when the limo breaks down.

—OPRAH WINFREY, TV TALK SHOW HOST, ACTOR, PRODUCER

When I have a problem, [my best friend] doesn't tell me what to do. She just says things that help me make the right decisions.

—ALECIA ELLIOTT, SINGER

You know everything about the other. You are comfortable. There are no secrets.

— JENNIFER ANISTON, ACTOR

Choose your friends by their character and your socks by their color. Choosing your socks by their character makes no sense, and choosing your friends by their color is unthinkable.

— ANONYMOUS

As my success has grown, I've really learned who my true friends are.

— JAMIE-LYNN SIGLER, ACTOR

Our closest girlfriends will remain constant, ready to tell us, whenever we need to hear it, that we're strong and good and equal to each new challenge.

— SANDY SHEEHY, JOURNALIST

Phyllis

You knew me when I didn't know myself
And when I lose myself you find me.
Whenever things get bad,
And I forget the good I've had,
You help remind me.

I tell you of my joys. My joys increase.
I tell my sorrows. They diminish.
And when I want to quit
You keep me going, bit by bit,
Until I finish.

Friendship is an art and you have made
The act of friendship your great art form.
I know that I can bear
The biggest chill because you're there

To keep my heart warm.

—FROM *SAD UNDERWEAR AND OTHER COMPLICATIONS*
BY JUDITH VIORST

Quick List: Top 10 Qualities in a Friend

According to *Get Real! Girls Speak Out About Everything* by
Lori Stacy, these are the most coveted traits in a friend:

1. Trustworthiness
2. Honesty
3. Friendliness
4. Sense of humor
5. Caring
6. Fun
7. Loyalty
8. Positive attitude
9. Understanding
10. Reliability (being there for you)

Chapter 6

All About You

You've probably heard the saying that if you want a friend, you've got to be a friend.

It may be a simple truth, but it's easier said than done. Being a friend is an art. And even the most devoted gal buddy can usually sharpen some of the items in her friendship toolbox.

Pretend you're witnessing your own memorial service, and imagine what people are saying about you. Are they gushing about how you were the most incredible companion, going out of your way to help them in times of need, staying in touch, making them feel honored and loved?

If not, here are tips on how to be the friend of your friends' dreams.

Cool Quotes

We are born into our families, but we earn our friendships.

—REBECCA STEFOFF, WRITER, EDITOR

You show people what you're willing to fight for when
you fight for your friends.

—HILLARY RODHAM CLINTON, U.S. SENATOR

Think of your friend as a precious piece of Ming jade,
or a rare ruby—something you can't afford to break
or lose.

—MARY ANN PLUNKETT, RECEPTIONIST

It is wise to apply the oil of politeness to the mecha-
nism of friendship.

—SIDONIE-GABRIELLE COLETTE, WRITER, 1873–1954

I didn't always have friends so I'm careful to take care of them.

—LORETTA CLAIBORN, SPECIAL OLYMPICS ATHLETE

There is nothing I would not do for those who are really my friends.

—JANE AUSTEN, WRITER, 1775–1817

Wear a smile and have friends; wear a scowl and have wrinkles. What do we live for if not to make the world less difficult for each other?

—GEORGE ELIOT (PEN NAME OF MARY ANN EVANS),
WRITER, 1819–1880

Let no one ever come to you without leaving better and happier.

—MOTHER TERESA, NUN, HUMANITARIAN, 1910–1997

Back from the Brink

My best friend Fred's mom and dad had been fighting. His dad attempted to commit suicide, but Fred stopped him. His mom and dad split up, and Fred started on a downward spiral.

He was always depressed and never wanted to do anything. I got him out of the house and around other people, but he was still down. One day I sat him down and asked what I could do to cheer him up. He said I had already saved his life—that my just being around for him had prevented him from committing suicide himself.

Now his parents are trying to work things out. While I wouldn't wish what he's been through on anyone, something good came out of it: We're the best of friends, and I know we can take on anything else the world throws at us.

—SARAH CARNES, 15

Chapter 7

Little Friends, Big Fun

Your childhood friendships are important. In fact, years from now they could be the ones you look back on in awe.

Why? When you're young, you're more open to making friends and throwing yourself wholeheartedly into being with them. There's also a lot of time—hours and hours to spend with them goofing off at sleepovers, dreaming up harebrained schemes, exploring the nooks and crannies of your house or apartment, playing sports, and stargazing. All of that activity can bring two people so close that they almost feel like one "unit."

This doesn't mean you won't have fantastic friendships later. But some of them may be different because people are busy with their adult lives, doing things like working and raising kids.

Whew—there's still plenty of time to be a girl and play! Track down your friends and get busy making memories.

Cool Quotes

They *are* love, those rare, binding early friendships.

— ANNE RIVERS SIDDONS, WRITER

Even where the affections are not strongly moved by any superior excellence, the companions of our childhood always possess a certain power over our minds.

— MARY SHELLEY, WRITER, 1797–1851

The music of those first friendships is always playing somewhere in the background as we go to other dances, other parties.

— LOIS WYSE, PHOTOGRAPHER, WRITER

There's nothing that can ever take the place of someone who knew you [when you were young] and likes
you, loves you, in spite or because of it. When that
someone is a part of the present, then you have the
rarest of all friendships; you speak your own language,
a kind of shorthand only available to childhood
friends.

— JILL MCCORKLE, WRITER

Swing Out, Sisters

In my best friend's front yard was a gigantic tree with
a canopy of leaves that seemed to block out the rest
of the world. Two swings hung from the high
branches. We would swing for hours, imagining that
our swings were rides in an amusement park, jerking
the ropes around for special effects. I would throw my
head back and feel the air rush across my face as my

friend jerked the swing left and right and pushed it up as high as her ten-year-old body could. Afterward, we'd sit on our respective swings and twirl ourselves around so that the ropes crossed in front of our faces. Then we would lift our feet off the ground and the swings would snap back into their original positions. Rule number one for swings: You always come back. The same is true with good, strong friendships.

—MEGAN CONDIT, COLLEGE STUDENT

Low-Maintenance Friends

"Don't sit there!" I cried. "Can't you see that Bob's there?"

It was really hot on the bus and I wanted the whole seat to myself. Noa gave me a weird look and tried to sit by my friend Laura.

"Alice is sitting in that seat, Noa!" she cautioned.

We started laughing and Noa joined in. We'd just met Bob and Alice, our imaginary friends.

From then on, two seats on the bus were always reserved for them. They joined all the games we played and helped us think of ideas for projects, do math homework, and answer essay questions. They were also good listeners, hearing out all our complaints. They were great to be around.

This happened in elementary school, but I'll never forget Bob and Alice. In a way, I miss them.

—DENISE LAU, 13

FRIENDLY FACT

Making friends during the school years can help a person develop good relationships later in life.

Quick List: Girlhood Favorites

What do you remember doing with your chums when you were younger? Here are some things that girls and women recall:

- Digging giant holes on the beach
- Hiding a sister's belongings
- Starting a spaghetti food fight
- Playing Monopoly and giving the loser money
- Making a cake but eating most of the batter
- Dressing up in Mom's clothes
- Convincing a sibling to go down the laundry chute
- Writing plays, making costumes, and performing for the neighbors
- Giving Barbie a haircut
- Two words: silly string

Chapter 8

Three's a Crowd

 *The apple of your eye, the other pea in your pod, the rhyme to your reason, your better half. Do any of these descriptions even begin to capture how you feel about your best friend?*

Probably not. But if you have a best friend, you don't need this book to explain it for you; you've experienced firsthand that giddy feeling of floating while at the same time being grounded in total comfort. You and your friend somehow belong to each other. It's hard to imagine life without her, and you've never had so much fun.

If you don't have a best friend right now, don't worry. Keep an open mind and heart. Remember, you only need one best friend!

Cool Quotes

Every so often you run into someone from your tribe,
a magic person.

—CARRIE FISHER, ACTOR

Many people will walk in and out of your life,
But only true friends will leave footprints in your heart.

—ELEANOR ROOSEVELT, FIRST LADY, HUMANITARIAN,
1884–1962

There is one friend in the life of each of us who seems
not a separate person, however dear and beloved, but
an expansion, an interpretation, of one's self, the very
meaning of one's soul.

—EDITH WHARTON, WRITER, 1862–1937

You're terrific as far as *I'm* concerned, and that's what counts. You're my best friend, and *I* think you're sensational.

> —CHARLOTTE THE SPIDER TO WILBUR THE PIG IN
> *CHARLOTTE'S WEB* BY E. B. WHITE

Once in a blue moon there's someone who knows it all, someone who knows and accepts you unconditionally.

> —JILL MCCORKLE, WRITER

So closely interwoven have been our lives, our purposes, and experiences that, separated, we have a feeling of incompleteness—united, such strength of self-association that no ordinary obstacles, differences, or dangers ever appear to us insurmountable.

> —ELIZABETH CADY STANTON, SUFFRAGIST, WRITER,
> SOCIAL REFORMER, 1815–1902

As a child, my number one best friend was the librarian in my grade school. I actually believed all those books belonged to her.

—ERMA BOMBECK, WRITER, HUMORIST, 1927–1996

Best friend, my well-spring in the wilderness!

—GEORGE ELIOT (PEN NAME OF MARY ANN EVANS), WRITER, 1819–1880

The Keeper

It was the end of our last year in junior high, and my friend and I were hanging out at McD's, eating sundaes. We reminisced about the past year—how we'd gone from shooting one another evil glares across the classroom to chatting over ice cream. We talked about how sad and scared we were to be leaving junior high and parting ways. The topic soon turned to people, and guys.

I can't remember who came up with the idea of guessing one another's crush, I just remember sitting there thinking, "I know who it is."

In a hushed voice, I half asked, half stated: "It's Tom* isn't it?"

I watched triumphantly as her eyes widened and her hand covered her open mouth. She was absolutely shocked. No way could she guess my crush. I'd worked way too hard to keep it a secret, and not even my two best friends from elementary school knew. She leaned over the table and said, "Steven."*

My cheeks flamed and my hands flew to my face. "Nuh-uh," I laughed, shaking my head, trying to convince her she was wrong.

"I knew it!" she practically shouted.

*Boys' names changed to protect them from "inflated head" syndrome.

Then in one squeaky, simultaneous voice, we asked, "How did you know?!?"

We collapsed back into our seats laughing. I looked across the table, over the melted sundaes to her, and thought to myself, "This one's a keeper."

—CHRISTINE SZETO, 15

FRIENDLY FACT

Boys are more likely to have groups of friends, while girls are more likely to have (one or more) best friends.

Chapter 9

Girls, They Want to Have Fun

With your friends, have you ever:

- *Played a joke and been in the vicinity to watch the effect?*
- *Played a game like charades or Pictionary for hours?*
- *Been kicked out of a quiet place because you couldn't stop giggling?*

If you answered "None of the above," get busy! It's practically a given that when gal pals get together they will at some point find themselves rolling on the floor in laughter. What else are friends for?

Cool Quotes

This much I know: If you can't look back and say it was great fun, then it wasn't worth it.

— DONNA LOPIANO, WOMEN'S SPORTS
ORGANIZATION DIRECTOR

Never underestimate the power of acting young and silly and crazy.

— CAMY BAKER, TEEN WRITER

My best friend and I laugh all the time. Usually it's for no reason—we just look at each other and BOOM, it's like an explosion!

— EUGENIE VALENTINE, 12

There is nothing like the sound of women really laughing. The roaring laughter of women is like the roaring of the eternal sea.

—MARY DALY, FEMINIST PHILOSOPHER

The best thing you've ever done for me
Is to help me take my life less seriously.

—INDIGO GIRLS, SINGERS

I can only be on my best behavior for so long. Then I need my rubber chicken. I need to laugh.

—CANDICE BERGEN, ACTOR

That is the best—to laugh with someone because you both think the same things are funny.

—GLORIA VANDERBILT, DESIGNER

Laughter brings us closer to the real us—the lovable us, the happy us, the free us, the us others want to be around.

—TERRY LYNN TAYLOR, WRITER

Girls—they want to have fun
Oh, girls just want to have fun.

—CYNDI LAUPER, SINGER

Girls Just Wanted to Have Fun

My best friend Jodie and I thought we were so cool listening to Cyndi Lauper and Madonna. They were symbols of boldness and femininity for us, and we spent hours memorizing their songs and lip synching. We got my mom to film us dancing around dressed in our most extravagant clothes to Madonna's "Like a Virgin." Nowadays, since we live in different parts of the country, it's rare that we see each other. But when we do, it's like we're ten again, snuggling under her electric blanket and staying up all night giggling, running around, and writing anonymous notes to boys at school.

—RACHEL KRAMER BUSSEL, WRITER

The Shortest Story

One of my friends and I were up for a starring role that was to be given to the shortest person. I was the shortest, and, in my eyes, perfect for the part. When my friend Sally got it instead, I was furious. She kept talking about it, which made me feel worse. At that point I did a stupid thing: I complained to Maggie, who told other people, and eventually the whole world knew. Sally and I were both upset. The next day we were alone together before rehearsing, and we broke into apologies. After that we laughed for a long time about anything and everything. Laughing is always a relief, especially after a touchy conversation!

—BLAIR REVERCOMB, 12

Quick List: Slumber Party Etiquette

- Do not invite someone who keeps saying, "Come on, guys. Isn't it time to get some shut-eye?"
- Two words: (1) junk and (2) food.
- Don't bother playing that trick where you dip someone's hand in warm water; it never works, and you always spill the water. The shaving-cream trick usually works okay, though.
- Make *sure* you know whether the other kids will be sleeping in pajamas, nightgowns, or the clothes they were already wearing.
- Plan on everyone being in tears at some point.
- Remember that the same person who keeps wanting

everyone to get some shut-eye will also be the same person who tries to wake everyone up early the next morning. Again, do not invite this person.

- Screaming during the ghost stories is a good way to make the next-door neighbors call the police.
- A ghost-story-teller is always lying when s/he says s/he knows the person the ghost story happened to. Nor does s/he know the "friend of a friend" it happened to.
- You do not have to pay attention when the host's parents come down and yell at you. At least not the first three times.
- Even though your parents say they won't mind if you call them at 3 A.M. and want a ride home, they *will* mind.

—FROM *1,003 GREAT THINGS ABOUT FRIENDS*, BY LISA BIRNBACH, ANN HODGMAN, AND PATRICIA MARX

FRIENDLY FACT

In a survey asking women what attracted them to their friends, a sense of humor won out over shared interests, kindness, and other qualities.

Chapter 10

Cel . . . e . . . bra . . . tion!

You probably look forward to celebrating your birthday each year, and the birthdays of your friends. You may observe St. Patrick's Day, the Fourth of July, Thanksgiving, religious holidays, and, of course, Groundhog Day. But what about Friendship Day, the first Sunday in August? Do you celebrate that?

It's not too late to start. You can do your part to commemorate it by honoring those friends that you hold most dear. Let them know you value their company—and their very being—as often and in as many ways as possible. Circle the day you met on your calendar and send them friendship anniversary cards. Surprise them with handpicked flowers, homemade cupcakes, and hearty hugs.

Happy Friendship Day!

Cool Quotes

Even the simplest shared rituals strengthen female friendship's bond.

—SANDY SHEEHY, JOURNALIST

When I am with my friends, it is a celebration of one another, of openness.

—CLAUDIA VANGERVEN, PROFESSOR

Take care of friendships, hold people you love close to you, take advantage of birthdays to celebrate fiercely.

—PATTI LABELLE, SINGER

I'm a big believer in toasting people at birthdays . . . toasting their great qualities, their friendship, their wisdom, their uniqueness. What could be better than being told out loud in a genuine way, with other people listening, that you are loved, respected, needed, appreciated, and adored?

—MARIA SHRIVER, TV REPORTER, WRITER

Celebrating Spring Break "Alone"

During my semester abroad in Ecuador, six friends and I, all women, traveled to the Ecuadorian coast for spring break. Everywhere we went, people asked if we were alone. At first we were confused by the question: "All seven of us?" We soon realized that Ecuadorian culture sees any group of women, no matter how large, as "alone" when not accompanied by a man. But alone as we were, we couldn't possibly have had more fun.

We enjoyed whole days on the beach. We spent cool, breezy afternoons lying in hammocks overlooking the water. Some evenings we danced in the streets, and others we talked late into the night. Every moment brought new laughs and challenges and pulled us closer together. Together we overcame the nastiest bathroom we'd ever seen, nurtured the sunburned among us, and proved them all wrong: We weren't alone, we were in the best of company!

—MEGAN CONDIT, COLLEGE STUDENT

Pal Project: Mark a Friendship Anniversary

An anniversary card is a great start; a gift is even better. Here's an idea for one that will keep on giving every day your friend looks at it.

Get a wall frame with a matte that holds two pictures side by side. Put a picture of you in one and of your friend in the other. Using pencil, write on the matte some or all of these things:

• Your favorite quotes about friendship
• The friendship code words that crack you up
• Words that define your relationship
• A greeting (as if you're writing her a notecard)

When you're satisfied with how the words look, write over them with black, metallic, or colored pens. Put the glass over the top and voila! A memento that's likely to stay on her wall for many anniversaries to come.

FRIENDLY FACT

February is International Friendship Month.

Chapter 11

Excellent Adventures

 *In movies, on TV, and in books, friendship and adventure go hand in hand. In* The Wizard of Oz, *Dorothy and her friends explore the Yellow Brick Road.* Buffy the Vampire Slayer *and her buddies specialize in brave feats. And let's not forget the creativity of the sister-friends in* Little Women.

You can fuse friendship and adventure in your own life. Being adventurous together is one step beyond having fun. It's a matter of being spontaneous and open to opportunities, for example, the chance to take a group night hike under the full moon, volunteer with a local environmental group, or make a haunted house for Halloween.

You're off to see the wizard. . . .

Cool Quotes

Anything, everything, little or big becomes an adventure when the right person shares it.

—KATHLEEN NORRIS, POET

I like trying things that are scary because you have never done them before. That really appeals to me; it is part of the adventure.

—RENEE ZELLWEGER, ACTOR

I love to go mud riding with my friends. We throw on old clothes and ride around in a four wheeler. It's so crazy and dirty.

—ALECIA ELLIOTT, COUNTRY SINGER

A Campy Story

One summer, my friend Teri and I decided to go on our first trip without adults. We packed up my car, complete with boom box (the car stereo didn't work) and *everything* we might need for camping. We headed from California to Arizona and Utah, camping at every national park we could find.

We were amazed that we never got sick of each other and always seemed to want to do the same things at the same time. (And people say traveling together is hard?) On our last day we didn't want to leave, so we pushed it till 10 P.M., had a barbecue, and then started on the fourteen-hour drive home. Somewhere in the middle of the desert the sun came up, and we were so tired that we stopped and took naps sitting up.

We came home completely fulfilled because we had

done this on our own and shared such special experiences. It was exhilarating to go wherever we wanted and know that we could take care of ourselves wherever we ended up!

—SARAH LONGAKER, BLOOD BANK RECRUITMENT MANAGER

Chapter 12

Tokens of Affection

 *Have you ever received a really cool gift from a friend? No, not something like a CD or a cute stuffed animal, or even a singing telegram. Something from the person's mind or heart that could have a far-reaching impact on you, such as a brilliant idea, encouragement, insight, a connection to someone who could help you, or a suggestion that never occurred to you.*

Maybe it's you who's given this kind of gift to someone. Maybe you've told a friend about a lead for a summer job that she landed and loved, or you helped her get up the courage to try out for the softball team and now she's the star.

Whether or not your friends are able to benefit, it's the giving that counts. Once in a while you may get lucky and see one of your gifts put to use. That's one reward that's hard to beat.

Cool Quotes

If your experiences would benefit anybody, give them to someone.

—FLORENCE NIGHTINGALE, NURSE, REFORMER, 1820–1910

I have learned that to have a good friend is the greatest of God's gifts, for it is a love that has no exchange for payment.

—FRANCES FARMER, ACTOR, 1914–1970

I never think of what others might do for me without giving equal thought to what I might do for them.

—JOLINE GODFREY, ENTREPRENEUR,

GIRLS ORGANIZATION FOUNDER

My gift to myself and my friends is my encouragement that they, too, are their own best selves.

—OPRAH WINFREY, TV TALK SHOW HOST, ACTOR, PRODUCER

She is a friend to my mind. She gathers me. The pieces I am, she gathers them and gives them back to me all in their right order.

—TONI MORRISON, WRITER

When I give a favorite book to a friend . . . I get a thrill when I think of them enjoying something I love so much—it's like giving the gift of a vacation to a whole new place.

—SUSAN BRANCH, WRITER, ARTIST

Kind words can be short and easy to speak, but their echoes are truly endless.

—MOTHER TERESA, NUN, HUMANITARIAN, 1910–1997

The Gift of Life

I was seventeen the summer I went with a group of teens and two leaders to snow camp on Lyell Glacier, far above Yosemite Valley. On the day we planned to climb to the peak of Mt. Lyell, we crunched up past the snowfield toward the last few hundred feet of the rocky summit.

After climbing for a while, I stopped to catch my breath, perching on an outcropping above the glacier to enjoy the enormous vistas. Suddenly, from out of nowhere, my friend Ian rushed over, threw himself at me, and we both smacked up against the mountainside.

A split second later, a huge boulder came crashing down, smashing the rock where I had been sitting. It flew past, bouncing and splitting into pieces, rolling onto the glacier, leaving an electrical smell in the air. I turned to Ian in shock and burst into tears, suddenly realizing what he'd done. Far above us we spotted a boy from our group with his hands frozen over his mouth; he'd desperately witnessed the near disaster triggered by his stepping on a loose boulder.

Years later, Ian and I met at a reunion and hugged for a long minute. Ian loves to tell the story of the girl he rescued, and I love to tell the one about the wonderful friend who saved my life.

—ANNE LEWIS, WEB SITE MANAGER

Saving a Friendship

My friends and I were playing a game in the wave pool. Diandra was in the deepest part, waving her arms. Everyone thought she was out there as a new part of the game that she'd made up, but I had a bad feeling. While everyone else kept playing, I started swimming toward her, getting water in my mouth from the waves. I finally reached her and helped her get back to where she could touch the ground. She thanked me over and over.

Our other friends rushed over, and when Diandra got her breath back, she told them what had happened—she'd gotten a cramp from swimming too soon after lunch and was in trouble. Since then we have been best friends.

—JANELLE MEEDS, 13

Pal Project: Make Cool Holiday Presents

Instead of waiting till the last minute and then rushing out to the mall with the crowds, why not plan a gift-making get-together with your friends? Here are a few ideas to get your creative juices flowing:

- Earrings
- Collaged "friendship boxes"
- Spa basket (with goodies like lotion and nail polish)
- Hand-knitted scarfs or caps
- Unique cookies or candy
- Handmade stationery
- Candles
- Beaded necklaces or bracelets in a friend's favorite colors
- Ceramic mugs or bowls (from a "studio store" or take a pottery class)

Also check out *Best Friends: Tons of Crazy, Cool Things to Do with Your Girlfriends* by Lisa Albregts and Elizabeth Cape.

Chapter 13

Comforting Thoughts

 *Someone at school is spreading a nasty rumor about you. You broke up with your boyfriend. Your parents are getting divorced.*

At times like this, it's not just convenient to have a friend, it's essential.

During tough times, when it may be hard for you to imagine any kind of a positive outcome, a true friend doesn't provide just a shoulder, an ear, and a packet of tissues. She pours on the compassion. She gives you all-important perspective so that you can see that there are ways out. She reassures you that you'll get through this, too. And she stays nearby as you do.

Cool Quotes

True friendship is like phosphorescence—it glows best when the world around you goes dark.

—DENISE MARTIN, BUSINESS EXECUTIVE

The best way to mend a broken heart is time and girl-friends.

—GWYNETH PALTROW, ACTOR

Once in a while you need a good cry and to put your feet up. You need someone to say things like, "Are you all right?"

—ANNETTE BENING, ACTOR

[Friends] make you feel everything is going to be all right with the world as long as they are around.

—BESSIE HEAD, WRITER, 1937–1986

It's so incredibly comforting to know that as stressful as life can get sometimes, there's always a good friend just a phone call away who can calm you down and tell you that everything is going to be okay, no matter what happens.

—MILA KUNIS, ACTOR

It's the friends you can call up at 4 A.M. that matter.
—MARLENE DIETRICH, ACTOR, SINGER, 1901–1992

I always felt that the great high privilege, relief and comfort of friendship was that one had to explain nothing.

—KATHERINE MANSFIELD, WRITER, 1888–1923

My feeling is that there is nothing in life but refraining from hurting others, and comforting those that are sad.
—OLIVE SCHREINER, WRITER, ACTIVIST, 1855–1920

The Song of the Whales

My friend Terry, her sisters Kathy and Joanne, and I decided to celebrate Terry's birthday in Hawaii. Tragically, about a month before the trip, Joanne passed away during a routine medical procedure. After the shock had passed, we decided to take the trip anyway and use it as an opportunity to honor Joanne.

We went on one of those boat adventures, and it wasn't long before we spotted whales in the distance. While we silently said a prayer, Terry let Joanne's ashes flow through her fingers.

Within minutes there were whales all around— babies and adults—jumping, breaching, and spiraling. We dove in the water and under the surface, where we could hear them singing. The three of us sobbed with joy, sadness, and awe. We felt that Joanne's spirit had swum up to the whales and begun to play. Later, the guide told Kathy he'd never seen a display like that.

—TONI SHEPPARD, MARKETING SERVICES MANAGER

If I Can Stop One Heart from Breaking

If I can stop one heart from breaking,
I shall not live in vain;
If I can ease one life the aching,
Or cool one pain,
Or help one fainting robin
Unto his nest again,
I shall not live in vain.

—EMILY DICKINSON, POET, 1830–1886

Winter spring summer or fall,
All you have to do is call
And I'll be there,
You've got a friend.

—FROM "YOU'VE GOT A FRIEND" BY CAROLE KING

Chapter 14

The Ears Have It

 *Have you ever been in the middle of telling a friend something when you realized she wasn't listening, or was answering with "I have that problem, too," and then proceeding to tell you about it?*

The importance of genuine listening can't be underestimated in friendship (or any relationship). A true friend waits till you're finished talking, then asks follow-up questions. After that she might talk about her own experience and how it's similar to yours. But ultimately the focus is on you.

Then it's her turn . . . and your opportunity to win points.

Cool Quotes

The most called-upon prerequisite of a friend is an accessible ear.

—MAYA ANGELOU, POET, WRITER

Inspiring someone can be as simple as listening. . . . So much brilliance is lost upon those who have no ears.

—VÉRONIQUE VIENNE, WRITER

The less you talk, the more you're listened to.

—ABIGAIL VAN BUREN, ADVICE COLUMNIST

Never fail to know that if you are doing all the talking, you are boring somebody.

—HELEN GURLEY BROWN, EDITOR, WRITER, PUBLISHER

Listening, not imitation, may be the sincerest form of flattery.

—JOYCE BROTHERS, PSYCHOLOGIST, WRITER

A friend hears the song in my heart and sings it to me when my memory fails.

—*PIONEER GIRLS LEADERS' HANDBOOK*

A good listener is not someone who has nothing to say. A good listener is a good talker with a sore throat.

—KATHERINE WHITEHORN, EDITOR, WRITER

When one's own problems are unsolvable, and all best efforts frustrated, it is lifesaving to listen to other people's problems.

—SUZANNE MASSIE, SPECIALIST IN RUSSIAN CULTURE, WRITER

Being a friend means mastering the art of timing. There is a time for silence. A time to let go and allow people to hurl themselves into their own history. And a time to pick up the pieces when it's all over.

— GLORIA NAYLOR, WRITER, EDUCATOR

Just One Look

I don't talk about my problems with most of my friends; they don't seem to understand. Except my best friend. Even though she's a year younger, she has the sensibility of someone much older. One afternoon when I was suffering from "guy issues," we went for a walk. I wasn't sure if she'd understand my problems, since she wasn't interested in having guys as friends or "liking" them. But I decided to go for it.

I poured all the worries out of my heart. They had been bottled up for a while, and it felt good to have someone just *listen* to me. When I was finally done, I didn't know how she would react.

She stopped walking as if she were thinking, then gave me this look of total understanding and reassurance. At that moment, I knew everything was going to be all right, and that maybe my real problem had been not knowing whom I could go to for help. She took my hand, and we walked on in silence.

—SARA LaHUE, 13

Could You Just Listen?

When I ask you to listen to me when I hurt or have a
    problem
and you start giving me advice,
you haven't done what I asked.

When I ask you to listen to me and you begin telling me
why I should or shouldn't feel that way,
you are trampling on my feelings.

When I ask you to listen to me and you feel you have to
do something to solve my problem,
you have failed me,
strange as it may seem.

Listen—all I ask is that you listen,
not talk or do—just hear me.

—CONNECTICUT CRITICAL INCIDENT STRESS TEAM

Quick List: How <u>Not</u> to Listen

When your friend is pouring out her heart, there are certain key things you'll want to avoid:

- Tell her she needs to just get over it
- Say, "Are you done yet?"
- Snap your bubblegum
- See who's on the other line
- Answer the cell phone
- Change the subject

Chapter 15

Girl Talk

 Gabbing . . . chit-chatting . . . yakking . . . "girl talk."

It sounds insignificant, but conversation is the glue that holds female friendship together. Girls and women thrive on sharing and "processing" the details of what they are thinking, feeling, and believing. It can be the most mundane-sounding, everyday stuff, but if it's in your mental, emotional, or physical orbit, it's fair game.

Talking keeps friends sane because it allows them to "clear the air." It also keeps everyone informed. You and your friend exchange information and then each of you may take pieces of what you've discussed and process them with someone else. Soon, everyone is wiser.

Cool Quotes

Ah, girl talk. It's so refreshing to be with such cool, smart women.

—REBECCA GAYHEART, ACTOR

[My friends and I] would be happy in a junky tent in the middle of nowhere, because all we do is talk.

—MARY McCORMACK, TEACHER

I think that on "guy" sets there are pranksters, but on a "girl" set all we want to do is talk to each other and hang out in the makeup trailer.

—MEG RYAN, ACTOR

We have our own secret hobby, and that's stealing away to gab.

—MARIA SHRIVER, TV REPORTER, WRITER

Ideal conversation must be an exchange of thought, and not, as many of those who worry most about their shortcomings believe, an eloquent exhibition of wit or oratory.

—EMILY POST, ETIQUETTE EXPERT, 1873–1960

The way I look at it, there's nothing private—it's all universal. . . . Nothing's going to be solved if we don't open our mouths.

—ANI DIFRANCO, MUSICIAN

There is a definite process by which one makes people into friends, and it involves talking to them and listening to them for hours at a time.

—REBECCA WEST, WRITER, 1892–1983

A gossip is one who talks to you about others; a bore is one who talks to you about himself; and a brilliant conversationalist is one who talks to you about yourself.

—LISA KIRK, SINGER

A Common Language

The language of girlfriends! I have no idea what a doohickey is, but when Doris calls something a doohickey, I know *exactly* what she's talking about. Not only do we borrow one another's clothes, makeup, and other doohickeys, but we also have reached the point where we understand each other's language. Sometimes when we can't even express our pain, the language of a girlfriend goes beyond what can be uttered. After all, the lexicon for girlfriends isn't entirely filled with words. Through its bulk of pages you will also see snorts, hugs, and tears. In this language there are even moments of no language, just silence. This silence is filled with understanding and strength.

—CHONDA PIERCE, COMEDIAN, SPEAKER, WRITER, RECORDING ARTIST

FRIENDLY FACT

In a survey asking women, "What have you and your friends done together in the past month?" 90 percent said, "Had an intimate talk."

Quick List: Talk Topics

It's pretty unlikely that you and your friends will run out of things to gab about, but just in case, here are some ideas to keep you going:

- The state of your friendship
- Problems
- Fears, hopes, wishes, and dreams
- Your ideal guy
- Whether your crush is anywhere near that ideal
- The weekend
- How to help the planet
- What you see yourselves doing in the future
- Your favorite band's new CD

- Whether things would be different with a female president
- Cool actors and musicians

- If you had three wishes . . .
- Pet antics
- The hobby that makes you lose track of time
- A juicy little secret
- Nothing in particular—just stuff

Chapter 16

Dishing It Out

"Lose the purple eye shadow." "You should invite Mallory." "Are you, crazy? He's in seventh grade!"

Anyone can give advice (and just about everyone does). The upside is that it's rewarding when your suggestions truly help your friends.

On the other hand, advice giving can be a double-edged sword. If a friend asks for advice, she may not want to be told what to do; she may just want to vent. In this case the best approach is to listen and help her clarify what she wants.

How do you tell whether "advice is nice"? When in doubt, let friends come to their own conclusions. Read on for more advice.

Cool Quotes

The advice we give is usually what we would do or would have done if we had the chance, and the advice that's taken, if ever, is often what we wanted to hear in the first place.

—Phyllis Dain, librarian, educator, historian

Advice is what we ask for when we already know the answer but wish we didn't.

—Erica Jong, writer

In a [friendship], advice is a gift, not a command—and it can be returned unused if it doesn't fit.

—Letty Cottin Pogrebin, writer

The true secret of giving advice is, after you have honestly given it, to be perfectly indifferent whether it is taken or not, and never persist in trying to set people right.

—HANNAH WHITALL SMITH, EVANGELIST,
SUFFRAGIST, WRITER, 1832–1911

Advice is one of those things it is far more blessed to give than to receive.

—CAROLYN WELLS, POET, ANTHOLOGIST, 1869–1942

The real art of conversation is not only to say the right thing in the right place but to leave unsaid the wrong thing at the tempting moment.

—DOROTHY NEVILL, WRITER, HOSTESS, 1826–1913

If it's very painful for you to criticize your friends—
you're safe in doing it. But if you take the slightest
pleasure in it, that's the time to hold your tongue.

—ALICE DUER MILLER, WRITER, 1874–1942

Sandwich every bit of criticism between two layers
of praise.

—MARY KAY ASH, ENTREPRENEUR, BUSINESS EXECUTIVE

Candle for Your Thoughts

Mrs. Smith's fifth-grade class had made milk-carton
wax candles to give as holiday gifts. Unfortunately,
some of them looked like someone had dropped
them. One of my classmates, who'd spent very little
time on the project, ended up with the best-looking
candle, while another, who had worked the hardest,
had hers turn to mush.

Mrs. Smith called me into the supply room. "Danny's candle is so much prettier than Kathy's— I fear Kathy will be heartbroken," she said. Together we decided to have the class draw straws for the candles.

I was only ten, but Mrs. Smith had chosen me as her confidante and asked for my advice. It was the first time an adult had treated me as an equal. But guess who got a smushed candle?

—ALDEN (BOBBI) DEAN, POET

FRIENDLY FACT

When it comes to hairstyles and fashion, teen girls are more likely to take their friends' advice than their parents'.

Chapter 17

Lean on You

 *The word* support *can mean a number of things: to hold up, to serve as a foundation or prop for, to argue on behalf of, to promote the interests of, to keep from fainting, yielding, or losing courage.* Supportive *describes everything from nylons to lampposts, but perhaps it best describes what a good friend should be.*

In terms of friendship, being supportive begins with being there— as if you're on standby. Then it's whatever action your friends should take, whether you're perfectly healthy and need only the awareness that they're nearby, or you have chickenpox and need chicken soup. But on certain occasions, true to the definition of support, a friend should hold you up (literally or figuratively), argue on your behalf, promote your interests, and/or keep you from losing courage.

Here's some support for this idea.

Cool Quotes

People are like vines. We are born and we grow. Like vines, people also need a tree to cling to, to give them support.

—ELIZABETH KATA, WRITER

Some people go to priests; others to poetry; I to my friends.

—VIRGINIA WOOLF, WRITER, 1882–1941

[My friend is] one of those people who I know will always be there for me. . . . No matter what kind of mood I'm in, she can cheer me up.

—SARAH MICHELLE GELLAR, ACTOR

We all need the support of a few people who value us as individuals.

—GLORIA STEINEM, WOMEN'S RIGHTS ACTIVIST, WRITER

There's a kind of emotional exploration you plumb with a friend that you don't really do with your family.

—BETTE MIDLER, SINGER, ACTOR

Those who have suffered understand suffering and therefore extend their hand.

—PATTI SMITH, POET, SINGER

I'm at the age where I need friends to support me and keep me interested in my days.

—NATALIE PORTMAN, ACTOR

There's nothing like helping others to remind you that you're not the only one in the world with problems.

—MICHELLE KWAN, FIGURE SKATER

A Moving Tribute

For a long while I had an incredibly difficult time figuring out who my true friends were. That all changed when I found out my family was moving. I became kind of distant because I couldn't believe it. I would walk around in a complete daze, and insignificant things would make me feel upset or cry.

The people who I suppose were never really my friends just disappeared; they couldn't deal with the way I was acting. This left my true friends. They were there close every time I needed to talk, cry, or just be quiet. They are the same friends who've kept in touch and are always dropping me a line to make sure I'm okay.

Moving was one of the hardest things I've ever experienced, but maybe sometimes it takes something that difficult to discover something as valuable as friendship.

—LAURA DIAZ, 14

FRIENDLY FACT

Psychologists think friendship is more important in our lives than it's ever been. One reason: the "traditional" family with a mother, father, and relatives functioning as a support group is less likely to exist. Many parents are divorced, and family members and relatives don't typically live in the same place—an estimated 27 percent of kids live in single-parent homes.

Chapter 18

Friendship Homework

 *Who's the new hottie in homeroom? How tough will the geometry test be?*

You can learn these things from your friends. But that's not all. You can also learn important things about yourself.

A good friend generally has no vested interest in what you do, so she can be objective. Yet she knows you well enough to see where you could stand to break a bad habit or live up to your potential, and she's willing to nudge.

Twelve-year-old Kira Bush of Midlothian, Virginia, offers an example: "I used to be scared of people and how they would judge me. My friend helped me overcome this fear, find my shyness, and destroy it."

A friend is a teacher. Your assignment is to be receptive to what she helps you learn.

Cool Quotes

A friend can tell you things you don't want to tell yourself.

—FRANCES WARD WELLER, WRITER

There's always something to be learned from people. Whether they give it or you notice it [are] two different things.

—REESE WITHERSPOON, ACTOR

Friendship forms and influences our lives . . . our minds, our bodies, our emotions—*and* our lipstick color.

—AME MAHLER BEANLAND AND EMILY MILES TERRY, WRITERS

The way people come to really, really understand things is not from being told. It's from living them, close up, through a friend.

— WINI SCOTT, HOSPITAL COORDINATOR

Each person grows not only by her own talents and development of her inner beliefs, but also by what she receives from the persons around her.

— IRIS HABERLI, URUGUAYAN SOCIAL ACTIVIST

I cherish having friends of all ages, and the beauty for my young friend is that I'm not her mom or her aunt; I'm an older woman to whom she can relate differently than she relates to family.

— NAN YURKANIS, YOGA TEACHER

Friends will tell you the truths you need to hear to make . . . your life bearable.

—FRANCINE DU PLESSIX GRAY, WRITER

No person is your friend (or kin) who demands your silence, or denies your right to grow and be as fully blossomed as you were intended.

—ALICE WALKER, WRITER, POET

My friends have made the story of my life. In a thousand ways they have turned my limitations into beautiful privileges, and enabled me to walk serene and happy in the shadow cast by my deprivation.

—HELEN KELLER, WRITER, LECTURER, 1880–1968

I'd never try to learn from someone I didn't envy at least a little. If I never envied, I'd never learn.

—BETSY COHEN, JOURNALIST

From the rocking horse to the rocking chair, friendship keeps teaching us about being human.

—LETTY COTTIN POGREBIN, WRITER

Quick List: Things to Learn About Friendship

- If you have two best friends instead of one, the three of you always have something to talk about.
- Even local calls add up.
- In every friendship, no matter how close, certain topics should be avoided.
- People who are nowhere near your age can still be worth knowing.
- Friends can like you without having to invite you to every party they give.
- *Everyone* comes from a dysfunctional family.

A friend who is doing you a favor will not appreciate "helpful" suggestions about the best way to do it.

—FROM *1,003 GREAT THINGS ABOUT FRIENDS* BY LISA BIRNBACH, ANN HODGMAN, AND PATRICIA MARX

Chapter 19

Inspiration Station

Who inspires you?

Hope you said one (or more) of your friends.

You know, the one who gets you excited about going to basketball practice or revved up about designing a class float for the homecoming parade.

According to artist and writer Sark, you can tell if a friend is inspiring to be with because "you will feel lighter, happier and bursting with some kind of new energy. It can be quiet energy, and it may not reveal itself until later, but you will begin to recognize the feel of inspiration."

As an added benefit, when you hang out with inspiring friends, you become more inspiring . . . and then your friends get even more psyched!

Cool Quotes

Every human being has some handle by which he may be lifted, some groove in which he was meant to run; and the great work of life, as far as our relations with each other are concerned, is to lift each one by his own proper handle, and run each one in his own proper groove.

—HARRIET BEECHER STOWE, WRITER, SOCIAL CRITIC, 1811–1896

As someone once told me, "The attitudes of your friends are like the buttons on an elevator. They will either take you up or they will take you down."

—JOAN LUNDEN, TV SHOW HOST

We are not passive observers of each others' lives; we help each other live them.

—JANET F. QUINN, NURSE, PROFESSOR, RESEARCHER

There is nothing more thrilling than to see someone grow in front of your eyes.

—LOIS JULIBER, BUSINESSWOMAN

Our friends can rejuvenate us by just letting us be, or they may drag our tired spirits and bodies, frequently protesting, to a place (physical or mental) where we will be renewed.

—CARMEN RENEE BERRY AND TAMARA TRAEDER, WRITERS

On a Roll

One of my friends in fifth grade inspired me to do things I never thought I could, such as score 105 percent on a big math test. She was always working for what she wanted, and it amazed me how she got what she worked for. Like the time she wanted these flashy new Rollerblades that cost a fortune—for her it was chores, chores, chores for a month. But of course she got her Rollerblades and she was real happy. That's when I realized that I really wanted to get a good grade on the upcoming math test. I studied hard and I got what I wanted . . . and that made *me* real happy.

—VANESSA TAN, 11

Quick List: Flicks to Watch With Girlfriends

Are you in an inspiration rut? Pop one of these girl-recommended flicks—many of which focus on friend-ship—in your VCR and prepare to fire up your spirits.

Babe
Beaches
The Breakfast Club
Circle of Friends
Ever After
Fools Rush In
Girls Just Want to Have Fun
Now and Then
The Parent Trap
Sixteen Candles

Chapter 20

Secret Information

Maybe you played a trick on your little brother and he's still wondering who did it, and even your mom doesn't know. Perhaps you overheard a confidential conversation about a relative. Maybe you did something you don't want anyone to know . . . or do you?

Everyone's got secrets. Not all of them are meant for sharing, but it can sure be fun to reveal what you're keeping from the rest of the world. It feels great to get a secret off your chest. And then the two of you can laugh about "our little secret."

That is, until one of you tells somebody else. A word of caution: make sure the friend you tell can keep a secret.

Pssst . . .

Cool Quotes

For everything that's true
I turn to you.

—CHRISTINA AGUILERA, SINGER

Girls especially are fond of exchanging confidences with those who they think they can trust; it is one of the most charming traits of a simple, earnest-hearted girlhood, and they are the happiest women who never lose it entirely.

—LUCY LARCOM, ABOLITIONIST, POET, 1824–1893

Women's propensity to share confidences is universal. We confirm our reality by sharing.

—BARBARA GRIZZUTI HARRISON, WRITER, PUBLICIST

I find it extremely hard to keep a secret. . . . I feel weird inside if I know something someone close to me doesn't.

—JORDAN STORY, 14

Think twice before burdening a friend with a secret.

—MARLENE DIETRICH, ACTOR, SINGER, 1901–1992

There's something you feel inside when you trust someone—that you can say anything—and that's hard to find.

—LA'KESHIA FRETT, BASKETBALL PLAYER

No soul is desolate as long as there is a human being for whom it can feel trust and reverence.

—GEORGE ELIOT (PEN NAME OF MARY ANN EVANS), WRITER, 1819–1880

Trust is friendship and friendship is trust. Trust cannot be expected or maintained without friendship to back it up, and vice versa.

—SARITA D. JACKSON, COLLEGE STUDENT

"No More Handshake"

At my friend's elementary-school graduation party, four friends and I were talking. Suddenly I blurted out a secret another friend had told me. I instantly regretted it and tried to convince them it was a joke. A cold, sick feeling enveloped my body. I was extremely mad at myself, because I am usually a trustworthy person.

The person I betrayed found out and sent me a note that said basically, "I'm really mad. I thought I was your friend but now I don't think so." (Also we had this special handshake thing, and at the bottom of the letter she had written, "No more handshake!") I was hurt, but I could just imagine what *she* felt like. I wrote back, "I'm sorry, I'm sorry, I can't believe I did that! Please can we still be friends? I will never tell any secrets again!"

I finally convinced her to forgive me. I will never forget how willing she was to do it. She could have shut me out from her life forever. But this mistake cost us the gift of wholehearted trust, because she still doesn't completely trust me a year later.

Trust between friends is a treasure! Think before you speak. You don't know how precious friendship is until you lose it.

—Sarah F., 11

A Secret Warning

One of my friends wrote me notes about how she was going to commit suicide. She told me not to tell anyone, but I told my parents, who said to bring the notes to my school's counselor. My friend hates me now. But I know that I did what was best for her, and I hope that one day she'll thank me for *not* keeping her secret.

—KELLY HERRON, 16

Secrets

Anne told Beth.
And Beth told me.

And I am telling you.
But don't tell Sue—
You know she can't

Keep secrets.

—FROM *IF I WERE IN CHARGE OF THE WORLD AND OTHER WORRIES* BY JUDITH VIORST

Pal Project: Invent a Secret Code

Are you concerned that your most sensitive secrets will somehow find their way to the wrong ears and eyes? Disguise them in a "secret" code. For example, get together with the friend who's most privy to your secrets and come up with a symbol for each letter of the alphabet (e.g., stars, hearts, lines, lightning bolts). For more ideas on how to code your classified information, consult *Totally Secret! Every Girl's Guide to Keeping and Sharing Secrets* by Caroline Plaisted.

FRIENDLY FACT

According to a recent poll of teen girls, 51 percent said they'd told a friend's secret; 49 percent said they hadn't.

Chapter 21

The Good Fight

 *Friendship is generally thought to be easy, fun, and rewarding. Yet, as in other kinds of relationships, friends go through rough periods. Even best friends get on each other's nerves and have blowout arguments. Just because people feel comfortable together doesn't mean they always agree.*

The important thing about fights is how you resolve them. It would be a shame to let an argument break up a bond you've enjoyed for years. No matter how mad you feel, invite your friend to talk about it. If you at least try to understand her point of view, you'll feel better. What seems like a major setback could turn into nothing more than a blip on the screen of your shared history—and one that's made you feel even closer because you've worked through it.

Cool Quotes

I've had moments of not speaking to people, but that's the way it goes. Friendships—if they're true friendships—are resilient, and you bounce back, and having a falling-out just adds another layer to them.

—MADONNA, SINGER

Never go to bed mad. Stay up and fight.

—PHYLLIS DILLER, COMEDIAN

Really good people are few and far between—don't let them go because of dumb mistakes or misunderstandings. The best friendships allow for a little flakiness.

—MINDY MORGENSTERN, WRITER

When you have real relationships, as opposed to relationships that are put together and forced together, you're always going to have issues.

—LAURYN HILL, SINGER

Any test of friendship involves a choice. We can respond in a way that brings us closer together, or we can respond in a way that pushes us apart.

—SANDY SHEEHY, JOURNALIST

The only people who you should try to get even with are those who have helped you.

—MAY MALOO, WRITER

We are drawn to each other because of our similarities, but it is our differences we must learn to respect.

—ROBERTA ISRAELOFF, WRITER

I now know the power of the word, I now know the beauty of a hug, and I now know it's better to find peace than to be right.

—JULIA ROBERTS, ACTOR

An apology is the superglue of life. It can repair just about anything.

—LYNN JOHNSTON, CARTOONIST

We have indulged freely in criticism of each other when alone, and hotly contended whenever we have differed, but in our friendship . . . there has never been a break of one hour.

—ELIZABETH CADY STANTON, SUFFRAGIST, WRITER,
SOCIAL REFORMER, 1815–1902

Sad Underwear

Knock, knock.
    Who's there?
Someone with sad underwear.
    Sad underwear? How can that be?
When my best friend's mad at me,
Everything is sad.
Even my underwear.

—FROM *SAD UNDERWEAR AND OTHER COMPLICATIONS*
BY JUDITH VIORST

Chapter 22

Unconditionally Yours

 *True or false: Your mother is one of your best friends.*

For many girls, the answer is "True," and, of these, many peg mom as their best friend. It makes sense. She's raised you from birth and probably cares more about you than anyone. Of course, she's also your mother and acts like it at times ("Clean this disaster of a room, young lady!"). But that doesn't take away from your friendship and those times when she's the coolest person on the planet.

If you and your mother are going through a difficult time, hang in there. Treat her like any other friend and ask what's happening in her world. Invite her to have some hot chocolate or go for a walk, and then have some serious girl talk.

Three cheers for mom-friends!

Cool Quotes

We are together, my child and I, Mother and child, yes, but sisters really, against whatever denies us all that we are.

—Alice Walker, writer, poet

My best friend has known me longer than anyone, has been there for me through thick and thin, has believed in me more than I believed in myself. She's given me values, morals, love, compassion, and a sense of humor. She is my mom.

—Samantha Erin Griffin, 17

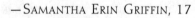

When life gets you down, and things start to close in on you, seek comfort in the arms of the one person who will always understand you even when you don't: your very own angel on earth, your mother.

—CHRISTINA CORNELL, WRITER, SPEAKER, COUNSELOR

[For fun] I do a girls-night thing—my mom is young, so I hang out with her and our friends. We . . . spend the whole night talking and making dinner.

—JESSICA ALBA, ACTOR

People are simply drawn to [my mother], and the friends she has are her friends forever—and then some. That's why I'm so lucky that she's my best friend.

—BRITNEY SPEARS, SINGER

Mom and Me . . . and L. P.

When I invited my mom to go camping with me, I discovered that she's a really fun person to be around. I remember watching her hang her L. P. (short for "little pillow") out on a tree to air "him" out. I laughed my head off because she was so silly. And I also realized, for the first time, that she was not different from me just because she was my mom—she was just another human being, one with her own vulnerabilities and more life experience. I saw her in a whole new light. To this day she's still one of my best friends.

—SARAH LONGAKER, BLOOD BANK RECRUITMENT MANAGER

Good Old Mom

Mom has always been a wonderful friend who's showered me with love and affection and has always been there for me. But when I was a little girl, I used to worry about her dying. When I was six, all my friends had moms in their twenties and thirties, and mine was pushing fifty. For as long as I could remember, she'd had a full head of gray hair. To a young girl this was conclusive evidence of her old age.

Since she was never ill, my concerns about her death proved silly. Today I have to laugh at them because Mom turned ninety-five this year. She lives with me, and I try to be as good a friend to her as she's always been to me.

—LUCY MURRAY, ARTIST, WRITER

Pal Project: Start a Daughter-Mother Reading Group

If you like to read, a nice way to get to know your mom better is to get together with your friends and their mothers to discuss books (every week, month, or quarter). Shireen Dodson, the author of a book on this subject, recommends that the girls lead the discussions. For information on starting a reading group, go to the library and get a copy of Dodson's book *The Mother-Daughter Book Club.*

FRIENDLY FACT

In a recent magazine survey, 95 percent of mothers said they felt close to their daughters and 42 percent said they were best friends.

Chapter 23

Oh, Sister!

 *If you adore your best friend, you might tell people, "She's like a sister to me."*

What if she actually is a sister to you? Thank your lucky stars (and your parents).

Maybe you don't consider your sis a friend right now. But wait till you get older. You and she would be ideal best friends because of your long-running history together and your common genetics. Just ask Internet expert Aliza P. Sherman. "My sister and I were mortal enemies most of our childhood," she recalls, "but recently I discovered that she is actually a really cool and generous person."

If for some reason your relationship doesn't improve when you grow up, think of how you could call a truce. The friendship sisters can share is simply too rich to write off.

Cool Quotes

In all the things we have shared—earache, chicken pox, measles, sweets, toys, books, love, ambition, shame, fear, to name a few, our two voices have been the most consistently shared.

—ELIZABETH JOLLEY, WRITER

Jamie and I have run the gamut from tearing each other's hair out when we were kids to ignoring each other to being each other's best friend.

—KELLY CURTIS, ACTOR, ABOUT SISTER JAMIE LEE CURTIS

Both within the family and without, our sisters hold up our mirrors: our images of who we are and who we can dare to become.

—ELIZABETH FISHEL, WRITER

Having a little sister is having a built-in playmate (and fan club, although you don't realize or appreciate it at the time).

—Sally R. Zanger, lawyer

The best thing about being a sister is the permission to be intimate—in short: *anything* goes. I have arrived at their doorsteps in complete need at various junctures of my life, and they have *always* unconditionally been there for me.

—Carol Wincenc, flutist

Family comes first, no matter how many times we play [tennis against] each other. Nothing will come between me and my sister.

—Serena Williams, tennis player,
sister of Venus Williams

You are always in the heart—oh tucked so close there is no chance of escape—of your sister.
—KATHLEEN BOWDEN (LATER KATHERINE MANSFIELD), WRITER, 1888–1923, WRITING TO HER YOUNGER SISTER

Whether we have sisters or not, we look for the archetype of the sister; the woman who knows us better than anyone, who shares everything with us, who loves us as a blood relative.
—CARMEN RENEE BERRY AND TAMARA TRAEDER, WRITERS

Sisters on All Sides

My big sister has not only been a sister to me, she's been there when I needed her the most, and this is how I describe a best friend. I'm also very proud of her; she is an awesome actress and singer. She gets into her character, and almost even becomes the character, and I enjoy helping her with her lines. She lights up my days at school when I see her on campus and she yells from across the field, "Hey, Margaret!" Unfortunately, next year she is going to college to study music and theater, and I'll rarely see her. But my little sister is coming along, and I hope I'll be to her what my big sister will always be to me.

—MARGARET CLINARD, 12

Stuck on You

When my sister Lynn and I were kids, we loved to play "save the world" games. One of our favorites was "Stuck-Together Twins." We pretended we were Siamese twins who would run out of breath if separated. Arm in arm, we navigated our apartment, stopping villains. Inevitably, one of us would run across the room and grab some "world-saving" item while we both gasped for breath. Together we were unbeatable.

Today, in our thirties, Lynn still helps me "catch my breath," offering advice on careers and relationships, celebrating my successes, and sympathizing when things aren't going well. She remains my "twin"—a mirror into myself. With her friendship, I am better able to face real-life challenges. It's fitting that the Latin word for "to breathe" is "inspiro," because as long as I have my "Stuck-Together Twin," I am inspired to overcome any obstacle.

—ELLEN BIRKETT MORRIS, WRITER

Sister, Can You Spare a Friend?

When I was nine years old, I had a friend named Emily. Since I had no brothers or sisters, I decided to call her "Sister." I remember playing hide-and-seek and calling out, "Sister, where are you?" I never did get a real sister, so that was the best I could do to alleviate my loneliness. However, it helped me form strong friendships for the rest of my life. I've always had only a few close girlfriends, and we think of each other as sisters in the truest sense.

—FRAN ZEINER, RETIRED PSYCHOLOGIST

Chapter 24

Built-in Buddy

 *What happens if your best friend is none other than good old you?*

This is obviously a different kind of relationship, but it's critical. Your inner friend can be there when you feel you can't trust anyone else, or when you have tons of friends but none are paying much attention. And even if you do have good friends, it's still essential to treat yourself like one of them.

Who knows? Another special someone may come along and assume best-friend status. But this is one time you won't have to displace one best friend for another.

Cool Quotes

I never realized what a decent companion I am to myself.

—DREW BARRYMORE, ACTOR

How many times and for how many years I have looked into the eyes of another . . . asking, "Will you love me?" Yet no one can give me what I have not given myself.

—JANET F. QUINN, NURSE, PROFESSOR, RESEARCHER

Often we try to blame friends for treating us badly or not providing the love we need. But ultimately, we are responsible for loving ourselves enough that our friends can't help but love and respect us, because we won't tolerate anything less.

—CASSANDRA WILLIAMS, YOUTH PROGRAM SPECIALIST

I'm content a lot of the time and I think it comes from taking the time to just be with myself, meditating, doing yoga, connecting with what's real.

— GWYNETH PALTROW, ACTOR

I read and walked for miles at night along the beach, writing bad blank verse and searching endlessly for someone wonderful who would step out of the darkness and change my life. It never crossed my mind that the person could be me.

— ANNA QUINDLEN, WRITER

If you listen to your conscience, it will serve you as no other friend you'll ever know.

— LORETTA YOUNG, ACTOR

When you're feeling your worst, that's when you get to know yourself the best.

—LESLIE GROSSMAN, ACTOR

When I'm with myself, I always have company.

—TRACY ROGERS, YOUTH COUNSELOR

I've become very valuable as a friend. . . . It started with learning to like myself.

—NATALIE COLE, SINGER

Don't wait around for other people to be happy for you. Any happiness you get you've got to make yourself.

—ALICE WALKER, WRITER, POET

Meeting a Friend in Europe

After college, I wanted to see Europe, but all my friends were busy in their jobs. I had just been laid off of mine and felt ready to go. Without even considering *not* going, I decided to go by myself. It was almost like I was "called" on this journey—I hardly thought twice about the decision.

Once I arrived, I had to rely on myself for every-thing—from figuring out directions, where to stay, and how to get there to changing money, getting food, and keeping safe. But I was lonely. There were times I thought I would die from the loneliness. My response was to be very quiet and go within myself.

Difficult though it was, this trip was one of the best experiences of my life. Why? By being alone for so long in places where most people didn't even speak my language, I learned to comfort myself. It was only by going through the loneliness that I discovered the friend I had inside.

—SARAH DEE, NONPROFIT ORGANIZATION MANAGER

The Perfect Friend

Today I found the perfect friend
who knew everything I felt.
She knew my weakness
and the problems I've been dealt.

She understood my wonders
and listened to my dreams,
She listened to how I felt about life and love
and knew what it all means.

Not once did she interrupt me
or tell me I was wrong
She understood what I was going through
and promised she'd stay long.

I reached out to this friend,
to show her that I care
to pull her close and let her know
how much I need her there.

I went to hold her hand
to pull her a bit nearer
and I realized this perfect friend I found
was nothing but a mirror.

—SHANNEN WRASS, STUDENT

Chapter 25

Social Studies

 *Are your friends mostly:*

    a. The popular crowd
    b. The jocks
    c. The nerds

d. People you love being around

If you want friendships that last, the best answer is, of course, people you love being around. Your choice of friends definitely shouldn't be determined by who's "in" and who's "out."

Later on in your life, whether you were considered cool in junior high and high school won't matter; what will count is whether you made great friends. So don't limit your social circle to any one group. Get to know anyone you find intriguing. When you and this person become popular with each other, you'll really have achieved something.

Cool Quotes

A lot of times in high school, people don't necessarily like their friends. They just hang out with them because they're afraid of being alone. Or they want to be with the popular crowd. But one really good friend is worth a dozen superficial ones.

—ANNE HATHAWAY, ACTOR

A popular girl is one who has many friends, or whom many people want to be friends with, but a friend is someone with whom you share secrets and intimate thoughts, someone you think of first—someone to whom you give priority.

—TERRI APTER AND RUTHELLEN JOSSELSON, WRITERS

If I make friends with someone, it's not because she wears cool clothes or hangs out with the most popular crowd in school. It's because of the way I'm treated and because I'm accepted, faults and all.

—DANIELLE FISHEL, ACTOR

In the long run, the girls who benefit most from the preadolescent popularity game are the ones who don't win it.

—SANDY SHEEHY, JOURNALIST

You can't do things based on what other people are going to think, because that's going to lead you nowhere.

—ROSE MCGOWAN, ACTOR

Friendship and Football

As a sophomore in high school, I'd finally found a best friend. But one day she told me we had to stop being friends: She had a crush on a football player and thought our friendship would harm her ability to get a date with him. She needed a way to join the "in" crowd, and it didn't include me. I was heartbroken.

Time went on, and other friends came into my life, including, in my senior year, the infamous football player. He and my ex–best friend had dated briefly. He asked why she and I drifted apart, and I told him. He said my association with her would not have made a difference to him or his friends.

I realized then that not changing who I was to try and join the popular group was the right choice. I lost my best friend, but I trusted that greater friendships and experiences would come along. And they did!

—ELIZABETH A. WHITTLES, PROGRAM DIRECTOR

Pal Project: Start a "clique Buster" Program

Eighth-grader Randi Pope of Long Beach, Mississippi, started a program known as "Circle of Friends." Kids signed a pledge to make all students feel valued and important, and they wore friendship bracelets to signify it. They reached out to people, taking those who had problems or felt left out under their wings. The program was so successful that Pope won an award.

For information on how to start a similar program, send a self-addressed, stamped envelope to teacher Dottie Warner, 204 North Cleveland Ave., Long Beach, Miss., 39560.

According to one expert, girls who have one or two close friendships turn out to be healthier psychologically than those who are widely liked but have no close friends.

Chapter 26

Boy Friends

 *Until now, the focus of this book has been on girlfriends. Hey, what about guys?*

Well, no, they aren't girlfriends of a different gender . . . and it would be boring if they were. However, girls across the country have discovered the joy of male company. There are lots of great reasons to have guy friends. Of course, you run the risk of falling in love with them, and if the romance doesn't work out, it could end the friendship. But this is a risk worth taking.

It's refreshing to be with someone who doesn't see the world the same way you do (as many guys won't). A male perspective can be helpful when you're agonizing about a love interest. And you may even feel more comfortable with a particular guy friend than you do with a girlfriend.

Let's hear it for the boys!

Cool Quotes

I need my men friends. I learn something from them that I can't learn from women, namely, what it is like to be a man.

—RITA MAE BROWN, WRITER

I've had men I've dated in the past say they're envious of my male friends because they feel like my male friends are always going to be in my life and they may not. From that point of view, friends seem to have an assured longevity.

—MADONNA, SINGER

My Friend "Thunderdome"

I don't know why it is so hard for people to believe that males and females can be best friends. Some people feel that having a best friend of the same sex is better because you can have sleepovers and relate more to each other. But I like the male-female relationship because it's less dramatic. Guys don't seem to be as sensitive about things as girls can sometimes be. When I tease Calvin and call him "Thunderdome" because of the enormous size of his head, he just calls me "Applehead" and we move right along.

—DESTINY HORNE, 13

A Friend Stands Up to a Boyfriend

I used to go out with a guy who was not very healthy for me; he would do things to hurt me or get me in trouble. My best friend, Ed, was concerned, but I wouldn't listen to him.

One night, Ed and I went out with other friends. As we were driving, we realized that my boyfriend was following us and trying to get us off the road. Finally Ed pulled into a parking lot, and my boyfriend followed and walked over to our car.

I could tell he was enraged with jealousy as he tapped on the window and started yelling at me to get out of the car. Everyone in the car was silent, and I started crying. He tried to grab me. At this point, Ed had had enough. He told my boyfriend that I was not getting out of the car, and that *he* would if he had to. My boyfriend stopped accosting me and just stood there as Ed drove away.

We didn't make it to where we were supposed to go that night. Instead, Ed and I went to Denny's and just sat and talked about what he felt and what I needed to do about my abusive relationship. That night, I decided I had been treated badly long enough, and that I would break up with my boyfriend. Thank you, Ed!

—NICOLE GRABOWSKI, 17

FRIENDLY FACT

In a *Twist* magazine poll, 80 percent of the girls surveyed hadn't dated a guy friend. Of those who had, 16 percent said it was a disaster, while 41 percent said it hadn't worked out but they were still friends. However, 23 percent said their friends had become boyfriends.

Chapter 27

Happily Ever After

Thirty years from now, will you and your best friend still talk on the phone every day?

It may be strange thinking that far ahead, but why not plan on keeping your friends for decades? Just imagine how great it would be to have them involved as you move in to your college dorm, celebrate your twenty-first birthday, pursue a career, meet the love of your life, give birth, become rich and famous . . . whatever you envision yourself doing.

Start building the foundations of your future friendships. Who knows how solid they'll become down the road?

Cool Quotes

Friends who grow old together can draw on a lifetime of mutual knowledge and shared experience, which is as great a treasure as any of us can hope to possess.

—REBECCA STEFOFF, WRITER, EDITOR

Constant use will not wear ragged the fabric of friendship.

—DOROTHY PARKER, WRITER, HUMORIST, 1893–1967

As we travel across the life span, *we make friends and friends make us*.

—LETTY COTTIN POGREBIN, WRITER

I expect that my women friends will be an even more important part of my life as I age. . . . We'll be like the crazy ladies who currently drive us nuts at public hearings.

— JOY MICHAUD, ENVIRONMENTAL SCIENTIST

Gentle ladies, you will remember till old age what we did together in our brilliant youth!

— SAPPHO, GREEK POET, DANCE AND CHORAL TEACHER,
CA. 610–580 B.C.

When I look into the distant future, I see us rolling into the sunset together. In our wheelchairs.

— CHRISTINA GARCIA, WRITER, ABOUT HER FRIEND JOSÉ

We have been friends together
In sunshine and in shade.

— CAROLINE SHERIDAN NORTON, POET, WRITER, 1808–1877

There's no friend like someone who has known you since you were five.

—ANNE STEVENSON, WRITER

Familiarity breeds content.

—ANNA QUINDLEN, WRITER

Party of Five

The five of us met in a support group when we were in our twenties. We've been getting together every month for thirty years, with rotating potlucks at each other's homes. We've been through so much and faced so many challenges together. We've shed a lot of tears and had a lot of laughs. Even though we've reached retirement, we still live within a few miles of each other. We think of each other as family—which is truly what we've become.

—MORREEN BEETLESTONE, ARTIST

Graduation (Friends Forever)

As we go on, we remember
All the times we had together
And as our lives change
Come whatever,
We will still be friends forever

—FROM "GRADUATION (FRIENDS FOREVER),"
BY VITAMIN C, SINGER

Shiny New Friends and Golden Oldies

Make new friends, but keep the old;
Those are silver, these are gold.
New-made friendships, like new wine
Age will mellow and refine.
Friendships that have stood the test—
Time and change—are surely best;

Brow may wrinkle, hair grow gray;
Friendship never knows decay
For amid old friends, tried and true,
Once more we our youth renew.
But old friends, alas! may die;
New friends must their place supply.
Cherish friendship in your breast—
New is good, but old is best;
Make new friends, but keep the old;
Those are silver, these are gold.

—ANONYMOUS

FRIENDLY FACT

Odds are that you'll live a long life filled with several long-running friendships. Female life expectancy in the United States is seventy-seven years, in Canada it's eighty-one years.

Chapter 28

Friendly Reminders

"Hello . . . Whitney? How are you?"

Although you might feel awkward calling a friend you haven't talked to in a while, you'll be glad you did. For one thing, it's essential to let your friends know they're still important, and to reestablish your connection. Plus, you'll be rewarded for reaching out: Even if you've been out of touch or physically far apart for ages, you and your friend will likely pick up right where you left off. And then you'll remember why you chose this friend in the first place: your excellent "fit." Presto, friendship tune-up complete.

Pick up the phone (or pen or keyboard) and get started on some friendship maintenance. It doesn't take much. Need a reason for getting in touch now? You're almost done with this book, and it's helped you appreciate your friends!

When you hear her voice, even over the phone, the bedrock of what you both know about each other pushes all that's real and true to the surface.

—KRIS KING, COMMUNITY HEALTH WORKER, WRITER

We should not let the grass grow on the path of friendship.

—MADAME MARIE THERESE RODET GEOFFRIN, WIT, SALONIST, 1689–1757

It's just a matter of really taking time out for friends. Even if it's two minutes, just to call and check in and say hey.

—CHRISTINA AGUILERA, SINGER

You should never say good-bye to a friend. Remember, friends are a lot harder to get than relatives.

—MARILYN VOS SAVANT, WRITER

I don't want to work for a while. I just want to rekindle my important friendships.

—RENEE ZELLWEGER, ACTOR

I'm a huge fan of e-mail. . . . I love it because your friends emerge as entirely different people.

—MEG RYAN, ACTOR

Nobody sees a flower really; it is so small. We haven't time, and to see takes time—like to have a friend takes time.

—GEORGIA O'KEEFFE, ARTIST, 1887–1986

I take time out for my relationships because those are the things that really matter. That's the stuff that's still going on when the lights are off, the doors are closed, and you're off the stage.

— CHRISTINA APPLEGATE, ACTOR

There is magic in long-distance friendships. They let you relate to other human beings in a way that goes beyond being physically together and is often more profound.

— DIANA CORTES, FINANCIAL ANALYST

The Write Stuff

Many people find that once their friends move away, their friendship fades. But I've found that distance has nothing to do with how you feel about a real friend.

You can share their lives and love them whether you live on different streets, or—like my best friend, Troon, and me—in different countries. When we met as teenagers, we were both passionate about one thing: writing. We planned to get an apartment together, get published, and be famous.

After twenty years we've both achieved our dreams of being successful writers. Helping each other along the way has been the best part, because sharing each step with someone who understands makes reaching the goal even more rewarding.

—SHELLEY BATES, WRITER

Face in the Crowd

Lalitha and I had been best friends for a year when she moved away. However, I'd resolved to keep our friendship intact, which was why, two years later, I was stepping off a plane in Atlanta, scanning the crowd for her familiar face. Worries tugged at me. Would we still get along? Our only conversation had been through letters and across phone lines—how would we talk in person? Suddenly a face appeared out of the crowd—those laughing eyes that had stared into mine as I'd shared my deepest secrets, the broad grin that had responded to so many private "insider" jokes. Suddenly I knew that nothing had changed in two years. We were, and always would be, best friends.

—JULIET LAMB, 14

You've Got Mail

I moved from Korea to America when I was eight. I thought my best friend would forget me. I know better now. She sent me a package about a week after I had moved into my new house. It not only had her letter in it, but five more notes and letters from my other friends!

This friendship still stays strong, held together by the letters we send. If you try, it's not hard to keep up a good friendship, even from halfway around the world.

—CHRISTINA PARK, 12

This Old Barn

Like the rafters of an old barn,
The roofbeams of friendship
Stay in place,
Held high and safe
By letters,
Our letters,

That protect us from the weathered world
Of time and space.

—FROM *FRIEND TO FRIEND* BY LOIS WYSE

Pal Project: Start a Friendship E-Journal

Go beyond simply pushing the "Send" button by documenting your friendship in cyberspace. Shanterra McBride of Lanham, Maryland, and her friend set up an e-mail journal when they realized how they had drifted apart over time and distance. "It has really strengthened our relationship," she says.

How is an e-mail journal different from simply sending e-mail? "We write in word-processing documents and then send them as attachments, which gives the journal a more permanent, purposeful quality," says Shanterra. This also keeps the e-mails from "scattering to the wind."

If you and a friend would like to start an e-mail journal, here are a few guidelines:

- Date each entry.
- Begin each entry with any comments you have about the friendship itself before delving into personal experiences.
- Focus on depth: feelings, reactions, and real life as opposed to the niceties of conversation/letter writing. It should feel as if you're writing in a journal that your friend happens to be privileged to read.
- Use the journal more as a record of what you're both going through than an exchange of advice or conversation.
- Include digital photos (your new haircut, the flowers you planted, etc.).
- Write entries at least three times a week.

FRIENDLY FACT

According to a SmartGirl Web site poll, 83 percent of girls cited seeing friends as a main reason they looked forward to going back to school.

Chapter 29

The Good Old Days

 Every good friendship has a few in its past: those profound, intense, or otherwise life-altering moments that are permanently imprinted in your mind. Something outrageous that happened at the mall. A time when you suddenly knew she loved being with you. The hot summer day you sat in the tree house and ate the whole carton of ice cream. When you were deathly ill and she gave you a giant card signed by everyone at school.

You know it's a special memory when you can recall the details—the way the sky looked as you watched a storm come in, what you were wearing, the grin on your friend's face, the feeling of being destined to be together.

"Remembering the past gives power to the present," says writer Faye Myenne Ng.

Remember when . . . ?

Cool Quotes

Here's an assortment of favorite friendship memories:

At the end [of *Romeo and Juliet*], when everyone was dying, my girlfriend and I were boo-hooing like every-one in the audience—and then I turned to her and said, "Look at her shoes, her shoes are really funny." And we started laughing and we couldn't stop.

— CANDACE BUSHNELL, WRITER

We'd set off for school side by side, our feet in step, not touching but feeling as if we were joined at the shoul-der, hip, ankle, not to mention heart.

— JAMAICA KINCAID, WRITER

Two of my friends and I had this huge pig-out with raw chocolate-chip cookie dough, s'mores, popcorn, Doritos. What else? Candy galore!

— MANDY MOORE, SINGER

We went ice skating until midnight. . . . None of us can skate and we just kept falling down, but it's fun to do dorky stuff like that with your friends.

— MILA KUNIS, ACTOR

[We'd get] our old running shoes on, and these flimsy air mattresses, and [we'd] just get on our cheap rafts and go down the river, laughing.

— ELLEN ALLEN, MOTHER

We used to sit with our arms around each other at the sunset hour and talk of our friends and our homes and of ten thousand subjects of mutual interest until both our hearts felt warmer and lighter for the pure communion of spirit.

—ANTOINETTE BROWN, MINISTER, 1825–1921

Jean and I grew up in the Big Band Era. We'd put a record on the turntable and practice jitterbugging in our scuffed-up saddle shoes. Much to the dismay of Jean's mother, we played Glenn Miller's "In the Mood" over and over. Then we fell across the couch, trying to catch our breath through the giggles. We were teenagers grabbing a small bit of pleasure at a time when grownups were facing the battlefield news and rationing woes of World War II.

—MONA TURA, WRITER

Swings

Memories start to fade
But always in their minds there will be
Two little girls in ponytails
Sitting on swings

—Lillian Schemadovits-Norris, 14

Pal Project: Make a Friendship Scrapbook

A scrapbook can preserve your favorite memories so you can return to them whenever you want, whether that's tomorrow or when you dust them off to show to your grandkids.

Rather than simply gluing your photos in an album, all the same size and all facing the same direction, put in a little time and do something more fun. Cut photos into shapes, use different-size pictures, glue them on colored background paper, add borders and stickers, and write what you remember about what happened. Craft stores carry all kinds of scrapbook materials. According to scrapbooker Vicky Langer, "It does take time and commitment, just like friendships do, but it's worth it. And working on scrapbooks together is a great way to grow your relationship."

Chapter 30

The Last Page

 *Now that you're full of facts about friendship, here's one last suggestion: Get out there and apply what you've discovered. Let your old pals know they can count on you. Say hi to new people and see what common interests you share. Plan a few adventures with pals both old and new, and always make room in your schedule for "girl time." Friendship is like an investment—the more you put into it, the richer your life will be. And your friends will love you for it, too!*

And we find at the end of a perfect day,
The soul of a friend we've made.

—CARRIE JACOBS BOND, SONGWRITER, COMPOSER,
1862–1946

Other Good Books

Check out these books for more friendship tips and stories.

CAMY BAKER'S LOVE YOU LIKE A SISTER: 30 COOL RULES FOR MAKING & BEING A BETTER BEST FRIEND, by Camy Baker (Bantam Skylark, 1998)

IT'S A CHICK THING: CELEBRATING THE WILD SIDE OF WOMEN'S FRIENDSHIP, by Ame Mahler Beanland and Emily Miles Terry (Conari Press, 2000; for older teens)

TEEN LOVE: ON FRIENDSHIP, by Kimberly Kirberger (Health Communications, 2000)

NEW MOON FRIENDSHIP: HOW TO MAKE, KEEP, AND GROW YOUR FRIENDSHIPS, by the New Moon Books Girls Editorial Board (Crown, 1999). New Moon also has a magazine—see www.newmoon.org

Copyright Acknowledgments

Index